# The Principle of Truth

By:
**Randy Williams**

MW00901268

Published by Melanin Origins

PO Box 122123; Arlington, TX 76012

Copyright 2022

First Edition

Library of Congress Control Number:  2021942163

ISBN: 978-1-62676-529-0 hardback

ISBN: 978-1-62676-530-6 paperback

ISBN: 978-1-62676-531-3 ebook

# The Principle of Truth

"I will always seek to know what is correct;
I will not lie or speak falsely."

www.MelaninOrigins.com

Good morning children. Today we are going to learn about truth and why being truthful is important.

1

The word "truth" is defined as a fact or a belief that is normally accepted by many people in society.

Telling the truth is important because it helps to build trust with other people. It is an important part of your character and who you are as a person; being truthful shows others that you are dependable.

People who are truthful are called trustworthy. Meaning, you can trust them with important information, people, and things. Actually, the greatest friendships are made once trust has been built.

As we learn more about the concept of truth today, we must keep in mind that being true to who you are is the most important part of this lesson.

Being truthful to yourself is the highest form of love and care. You should be proud of the person you see when you wake up in the morning and look in the mirror.

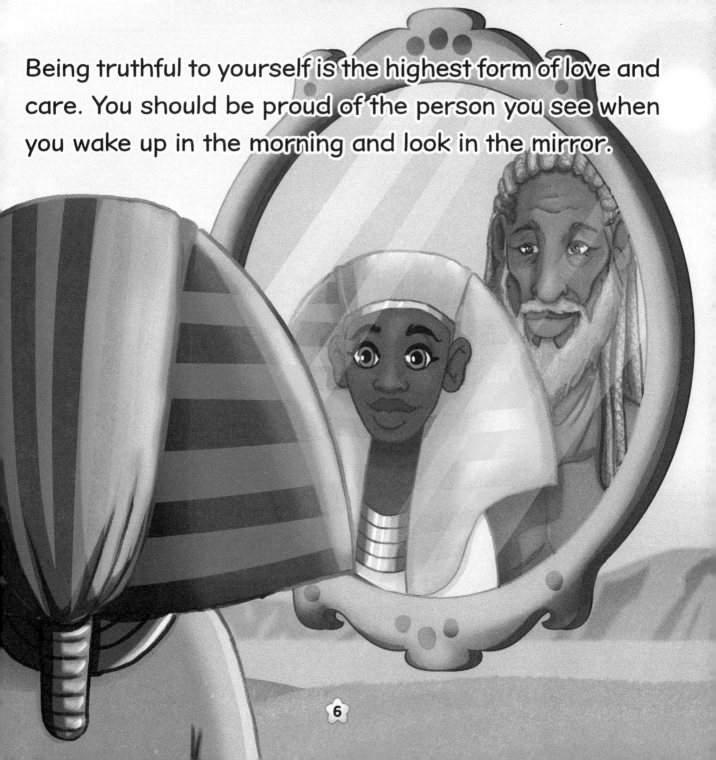

You should be happy and confident about who you are deep inside; a good way to feel this way is to tell the truth.

The truth gives us power to stand up for ourselves and be brave.

8

When we are not truthful, it causes us to feel sad and afraid.

There are benefits to being a truthful person. Most people are willing to help you in a time of need if they know that you are an honest person.

Show me a truthful person and I'll show you someone who lives by the core values of truth: honesty, integrity, and trustworthiness.

Honesty means your actions are truthful.

12

Integrity means that you value following the rules and doing the right thing even when there is no one else around.

13

Trustworthiness means to believe and depend on someone or something. It means someone or something is worthy of trust.

Practicing the core values of truth everyday helps to build friendships, create loving environments for all people to enjoy, and it helps us to feel better about ourselves when we know that we are giving our best effort to act truthfully.

Truth, alone, brings many opportunities that have the power to improve people's lives and the condition of their communities around the world.

If everyone in the world told the truth... the world would be a more beautiful place.

# Modern Day Melanin Origins

This book is dedicated to a mighty woman of truth: **Dr. Marimba Ani.**

**Dr. Marimba Ani** is an anthropologist and African Studies scholar best known for coining the term *Maafa* to describe the African holocaust.

A retired Professor of Afrikan Studies at Hunter College, **Dr. Ani** lectures nationally and focuses her attention on the urgent need for healing, warrior-training, and the creation of a sovereign consciousness among African people in the world-wide diaspora.

~ FAMU.org

CPSIA information can be obtained
at www.ICGtesting.com
Printed in the USA
BVHW021553091121
621174BV00019B/531

9 781626 765306